T0194064

THIRTY DAYS OF JOY

*A Devotional to Keep You Stirred
Up and Rejoicing at All Times*

MICHAEL G. CRENSHAW

WESTBOW
PRESS®
A DIVISION OF THOMAS NELSON
& ZONDERVAN

All scriptures are from the KING JAMES VERSION (KJV):
KING JAMES VERSION, public domain

WestBow Press books may be ordered through booksellers or by contacting:

WestBow Press
A Division of Thomas Nelson & Zondervan
1663 Liberty Drive
Bloomington, IN 47403
www.westbowpress.com
1 (866) 928-1240

ISBN: 978-1-9736-1961-1 (sc)
ISBN: 978-1-9736-1960-4 (e)

Print information available on the last page.

WestBow Press rev. date: 04/13/2018

THIRTY DAYS OF JOY
A DEVOTIONAL

Joy can be defined as a supernatural force from God that is a byproduct of the born-again recreated spirit that characterizes the victorious life.

DEDICATION

This book is dedicated to my wife of almost thirty years Phyllis-McCray Crenshaw for your faithful love and constant support. This project could not have been completed without your cooperation. You have always been willing to support the vision and direction that God has given me and I am grateful for it. From Birmingham, Alabama and even unto Cartago, Costa Rica you have been the perfect complement to my ministry. Many doors have remained opened because you and your gifts. May the Lord continue to cause His face to shine upon you mightily! I love you dearly.

Mike

DAY 1

THE JOY OF THE LORD IS YOUR STRENGTH

Joy what a concept. But it is more than just a principle; it is a supernatural force that originates from the born-again recreated spirit. To be more specific we can define joy as "a supernatural force of God that is a by-product of the born-again recreated spirit that characterizes the victorious life." Here is one of life's greatest

> The Lord gives us the key to dealing with the tribulation. He commands us to be of good cheer! He is talking about a living faith that rejoices until the victory is won! In spite of the negatives in life, always make a quality decision to be of good cheer.

keys to success and victory, a revelation to profound to ignore. The joy of the Lord is your strength!

The original Hebrew meaning indicates that strength means fortress, stronghold, place of refuge, a harbor. Joy is that place of refuge that protects you in a time of trial. Think about it. What do you need the most during times of testing and temptation? What is the first thing that departs from your spirit when bad news comes? Your strength, which is the same as joy according Nehemiah 8:10. The joy of the Lord is the supernatural force that gives you the ability to outlast the storm! I want you to notice what Jesus said in John 16:33.

John 16:33 (KJV)

[33] These things I have spoken unto you, that in me ye might have peace. In the world ye shall have tribulation: but be of good cheer; I have overcome the world.

Jesus taught that we would have tribulation, but He encouraged us to be of good cheer because He had overcome the world. Now many preachers major on the negative side of this verse. But let's major on the victory side! The Lord gives us the key to dealing with the tribulation. He commands us to be of good cheer! He is talking about a living faith that rejoices until the victory is won! In spite of the negatives in life, always make a quality decision to be of good cheer. If you do you will maintain your joy and you will outlast your trial.

Paul said to be "strong in the Lord" in Ephesians 6:10, Joel taught us to say "Let the weak say I am strong." Remember your joy is your stronghold and place of refuge. It is your spiritual gas mask that will enable you to endure and outlast the poisonous gases of life that seek to stop you from living the abundant life. Joy, don't leave home without it!

Scripture References

Nehemiah 8:10; John 16:33; Ephesians 6:10; Joel 3:10

DAY 2
COUNT IT ALL JOY

When things are well, count it all joy. When things are not well, count it all joy. When things look up, count it all joy, and when things look bad, count it all joy. Notice James 1:2 in the Amplified:

"Consider it wholly joyful, my brethren whenever you are enveloped in or encounter trials of any sort or fall into various temptations."

> You open your mouth declaring that God is bigger than your problems! Greater than your circumstances, and stronger than your foes! When you do this, you can shout your way out of depression, discouragement, defeat, delays and everything else that the enemy is attempting to put on you!

One translation even says to welcome tests and trials as friends! Counting it all joy is a quality decision that goes beyond the feelings of men. In spite of how I may feel I decide to rejoice in the Lord anyhow! This is how you get to the place where you welcome the trials of life. You make a bold confession, and then you rejoice in the Lord in spite of the test. You open your mouth declaring that God is bigger than your problems! Greater than your circumstances, and stronger than your foes! When you do this, you will shout your way out of depression, discouragement, defeat, delays, and everything else that the enemy is attempting to put on you!

Someone said that the most important thing is not what happened to you, but rather your reaction to it. My friend take the time to put the Word of God in your spirit, so when the storm comes (and it will come) you will have a firm foundation of faith that will anchor you. When the pressures of life put the squeeze on you, let the joy of the Lord be the only thing that comes out of you!

Scripture References

James 1:2; Mark 11:23; Job 22:28; Philippians 4:13

DAY 3

A CONTINUAL FEAST

Proverbs 15:15 states, "All the days of the afflicted are evil: but he that is of a merry heart hath a continual feast. The Amplified adds regardless of the circumstances. Praise the Lord! There are benefits to maintaining a merry heart. Don't settle for "Blue Mondays and Down Days." Jesus paid a tremendous price in order that we might live the victorious abundant life. The possession of a merry heart is a personal decision we make every day. God promises a continual feast. The idea in the Hebrew is perpetual, something that is indefinite. It also means to stretch! So in other words the person with a merry heart can stretch out the benefits of joy as long as he pleases. Jesus taught "according to your faith be it unto you."

Refuse to have pity parties! Stop feeling sorry for yourself! If you are a born again child of God you are blessed! You have the favor of God upon you! It does not matter what is going on in your personal life, the Word of the living God declares that you are an overcomer!

> There are benefits to maintaining a merry heart. Don't settle for "Blue Mondays and Down Days." Jesus paid a tremendous price in order that we might live the victorious abundant life.

1 John 5:4 (KJV)

4 For whatsoever is born of God overcometh the world: and this is the victory that overcometh the world, *even* our faith.

Learn to enjoy the simple things of life. Many of us are on the road to bigger and better things, but if you are not careful you will get caught up in building your own kingdom and eventually you will wear down. That's when the devil will attack, when you are at your weakest! So guard against the tendency to depend upon your own efforts. The Word of God declares that it is "Not by power, not by might, but by my Spirit, saith the Lord. (Zechariah 4:6). The Psalmist also teaches in Psalms 127:1 "Except the Lord builds the house, they labor in vain that build it." So sit back and enjoy life and remember a merry heart goes a long way!

Scripture References

Proverbs 15:15; 1 John 5:4; Zechariah 4:6; Psalms 127:1

DAY 4

SMILE A WHILE

There was a popular rock group during the seventies that penned the words "Smile a While" on one of their records. It is amazing what a smile can do for a room. It radiates joy and it warms the hearts of those who bask in its presence. Someone said "Life is like a mirror. If we frown at it, it frowns back. If we smile it returns the greeting."

> The person who never smiles or laughs sends a signal to the world that something is wrong. Nobody likes to be around a "sour puss!" People who live like this are most likely meditating on negative circumstances instead of living a thankful life

One of the greatest gifts you can give every day is a smile! It is free of charge and it will pay dividends back to the one who gave it. People will judge us by our looks and first impressions are lasting. The person who never smiles or laughs sends a signal to the world that something is wrong. Nobody likes to be around a "sour puss"! People who live like this are most likely meditating on negative circumstances instead of living a thankful life. I like what Paul said in 1 Thessalonians 5:18:

1 Thessalonians 5:18 (KJV)

[18] In everything give thanks: for this is the will of God in Christ Jesus concerning you.

In spite of what may be happening in our lives, we must learn to see God in every test. We must see his power to deliver, and to help those in need.

A smile is an indication and evidence of the inward working of joy. When you realize that you "always triumph in Christ Jesus" (II Corinthians 2:14)," that you are more than a conqueror" (Romans 8:37), and that we are victors in Christ, you understand the key to stress free living. For the happy heart, life is a continual feast. (Proverbs 15:15) Remember the world looks brighter behind a smile! So make life easier on yourself. It takes 26 muscles to make a smile and 62 to frown. The choice is simple, smile a while.

Scripture References

1 Thessalonians 5:18; II Corinthians 2:14; Romans 8:37; Proverbs 15:15

DAY 5

AN INDICATIOR OF FAITH!

Joy is one of the surest indicators of faith in a Believer's life. Where there is no joy there can be no faith, because a life absent of joy is often a life filled with doubt, unbelief, and anxiety. Paul said to the Romans "Now the God of hope fill you with all joy and peace in believing." (Romans 15:13) Notice that he coupled joy and peace with believing faith. The person devoid of joy and peace is one who has not entered into the rest of God. (Hebrews 4:10) I heard a preacher put it like this, "Faith rejoices and is glad, doubt frets and is sad." The person full of faith is excited about what the Word of God has promised! He knows that the Word cannot fail, so he is expectant, trusting God for His intervention and deliverance! That is true Bible faith. It is full of joy unspeakable and full of glory.

1 Peter 1:8 (KJV)

8 Whom having not seen, ye love; in whom, though now ye see *him* not, yet believing, ye rejoice with joy unspeakable and full of glory:

> The person devoid of joy and peace is one who has not entered into the rest of God....The person full of faith is excited about what the Word of God has promised!

Jesus said to believe that you receive when you pray. (Mark 11:24) If we really believe that we have received then there should be joy in our lives! Answered prayer produces joy, deliverance from bondages produces joy, and financial miracles produce great joy. So as you are strolling down

9

life's highway, keep your eye on two gauges. The peace gauge and the joy gauge. If you get low on one stop, and get to the service station quick and fill your tank with joy!

Romans 15:13 (KJV)

[13] Now the God of hope fill you with all joy and peace in believing, that ye may abound in hope, through the power of the Holy Ghost.

Scripture References

Romans 15:13; 1 Peter 1:8; Mark 11:24; Hebrews 4:10

DAY 6
SHOUT IT OUT!

We all remember the old commercial where the wife shouts out all the stains in the family laundry. Instead of wringing her hands in frustration over tough stains, she calmly declares that she will just shout out those stubborn patches of food, grass, and greasy spots.

> I guarantee that you cannot stay depressed and shout at the same time! Something has to give and it won't be your joy. Remember Jesus gave you something to shout about! So shout it out!

But there is a spiritual principle here. The Word of God encourages us to make noise with our voices of praise! Psalms 41:1 declares "O clap your hands all ye people shout unto God with the voice of triumph." Before the walls of Jericho fell, God instructed Joshua to have the people shout, and when they shouted, the walls came tumbling down. I know some will say, "I'm not the shouting type. I do love the Lord but I prefer to praise Him in my own way." That is why your way may be dark and gloomy. We must learn to follow Jesus's way or it may be the highway! When we realize that we already have the victory, our hearts will cry out with the voice of triumph. God's people must understand that there is a shout of a king among us.

Numbers 23:21 (KJV)

[21] He hath not beheld iniquity in Jacob, neither hath he seen perverseness in Israel: the LORD his God *is* with him, and the shout of a king *is* among them.

When the King of kings and Lord of lords is in our midst, there will be joyful shouting and exclamations of praise.

So the next time depression, gloom and doom, or discouragement comes your way, lift up your head and shout it out. Shout about what, you may ask? Shout about how big your God is! Shout about how great your God is! Shout about the blood of Jesus! Shout about the eternal Word of God! Shout about heaven! Shout about the fact that you are not going to hell! Hallelujah! The more you shout, the better you will feel and the faster the devil will run. Your depression and discouragement will flee also. So why not shout right now. Go ahead and try it! I guarantee that you cannot stay depressed and shout at the same time! Something has to give and it won't be your joy. Remember Jesus gave you something to shout about! So shout it out!

Scripture References

Psalms 47:1; Numbers 23:21; Joshua 6:20

DAY 7

BLESS THE LORD AT ALL TIMES

When is it a good time to bless the Lord? Is He only good when everything is fine? Is He only good when there is money in the bank, food on the table, and when we have a nice home or automobile? Is this the only time we can find it within ourselves to bless the Lord? No, David said we are to bless the Lord at all times. In good times or bad times, whenever and wherever, we should bless the Lord.

> Jesus is worthy of our praise! As we continue to walk with Him down life's highway, we come to understand His greatness and power. We also understand that He deserves our praise even when we don't feel like giving it. David said that God's praise would continually be in his mouth. In other words he was living a life of praise.

Jesus is worthy of our praise! As we continue to walk with Him down life's highway, we come to understand His greatness and power. We also understand that He deserves our praise even when we don't feel like giving it. David said that God's praise would continually be in his mouth. In other words he was living a life of praise. I believe that Paul has this idea in mind when He talked about presenting our bodies as "living sacrifices." (Romans 12:1)

One true mark of a mature child of God is how they handle adversity. James taught us to count it all joy when we fall into various test and trials. He did not tell us to ball and squall and wonder why me. He said the same thing that David said which is to bless the Lord. If we would practice giving

God the glory in the midst of our struggles we would experience genuine joy and peace. David and James are both talking about making a quality decision in spite of the struggles that face us. I heard someone teach that habit is stronger than desire. If we would learn the habit of blessing God, it would close the devil's doorway into our lives by cancelling frustrations and pity parties when things go wrong.

1 Thessalonians 5:18 (KJV)

[18] In every thing give thanks: for this is the will of God in Christ Jesus concerning you.

Scripture References

Psalms 34:1; Romans 12:1; James 1:2; 1 Thessalonians 5:18

DAY 8
STIR IT UP

Paul told Timothy to stir up the gift of God! (2 Timothy 1:16) In other words activate, bring to life, or arouse what God put in you! When we were born again we received the joy of our salvation. The joy that comes only from realizing that you are saved and delivered from the penalty of sin. A joy that's unspeakable and full

> But in reality the joy that God gave you is still there, it is just lying dormant. Here is where maturity steps in. You have to know that the supernatural force of joy is still yours and is still alive. It's faith without feelings, its belief without sight that works independent of the carnal perceptions of the soul.

of glory. (1 Peter 1:8) It's an everlasting joy, and eternal happiness that is ours for all time.

Now the devil will try to make you think that you have lost your joy. All of a sudden you just don't feel like you used to. The initial enthusiasm begins to wear off! It's like the new car or outfit, you are so excited when you first get it, but after a while you get adjusted and it's not the same anymore. B.B. King said it best in his song "The Thrill is Gone." But in reality the joy that God gave you is still there, it is just lying dormant. Here is where maturity steps in. You have to know that the supernatural force of joy is still yours and is still alive. It's faith without feelings, it's belief without sight, that works independent of the carnal perceptions of the soul.

Sometimes your joy is like the sugar in the Kool Aid that sits in the refrigerator for some time. You pour a nice cool glass but the taste is funny. What happened? Did the sweetness go away, should the rest of the Kool Aid be discarded? Heavens no! You just need to dip a long handled spoon into the container and stir up the contents which have settled at the bottom. Then you take a swig and guess what? The beverage now tastes like it did when you first mixed it!

It's the same way with your joy. Maybe you have allowed the hustle and bustle of life along with the trials and tribulations that are common to all men cause you to lose your focus on keeping your joy. Always remember that joy is a decision. So stir it up! Whatever you need to do to put you back on "joy junction do it. Sing a song, dance before the Lord, run, shout, or clap your hand. Do it! Stir it up!

Scripture References

2 Timothy 2:16; 1 Peter 1:8

DAY 9
FULL OF JOY

Full! What a word, what a concept! Related terms would be replete, brimful, overflowing, running over, abundant, packed, jammed, satiated, abounding. Friend, that is the nature of God, to do things big, and extravagant, in an over the top way. With this in mind we can understand why God wants our joy to be on this level also. Jesus made several statements concerning the force of joy, notice these two:

> Here is a point that I preach often and this will help you in this area. And this is it, "the size of your revelation will determine the size of your faith." Your revelation of joy will determine the amount joy you live in. So catch the revelation, you are full of joy and the victory is yours!

John 15:11 (KJV)

[11] These things have I spoken unto you, that my joy might remain in you, and *that* your joy might be full.

John 16:24 (KJV)

[24] Hitherto have ye asked nothing in my name: ask, and ye shall receive, that your joy may be full.

It seems like the Lord God is concerned about our joy!

Again Jesus said "I am come that you might have life, and have it more abundantly." (John 10:10) Can you imagine having life without joy? It would not be much fun that is for sure! No, thank God, the Lord wants us to be full of joy, overflowing with joy, running over with joy, satiated with joy. Make your confession bold by declaring that you are full of joy! Mark 11:23 teaches that we will have what we say, so say it often. Especially when things are going wrong, make your declaration and declare what you believe with your words! Every morning declare that God's joy is your strength and say "I am full of joy." People who are full of joy are excited, enthusiastic, kind, and beam with the glory of God in their faces! Here is a point that I preach often and this will help you in this area. And this is it, "the size of your revelation will determine the size of your faith." Your revelation of joy will determine the amount joy you live in. So catch the revelation, you are full of joy and the victory is yours!

Scripture References

John 15:11; John 16:23; Mark 11:23

DAY 10

GET A REVELATION OF VICTORY

One of the most important keys to living a life of joy is realizing your victory in Jesus. The Word of God says "God always causes us to triumph." (2 Corinthians 2:14) Notice it says always! Even in apparent defeat God can **cause** us to have the victory. Victory speaks of winning! God is a winner, Jesus is a winner and the Holy Ghost is a winner! This means that every born-again child of God is a winner whether they realize it or not. When Jesus defeated death, hell, and the grave, he conferred and passed on His victory to us!

Now it is up to us to get a revelation of our victory in Jesus and begin to walk in that victory in every area of our lives. Over and over the scriptures proclaim our winning walk as children of God. Paul said that "we are more than conquerors." (Romans 8:37) John said that "we are overcomers", (1 John 4:4), and Jesus said that we were "salt and light." (Matthew 5:13-16) Therefore in order to experience what God says is already ours we must understand or know what he has provided. Revelation has to do with knowing. The word revelation is derived from the root word reveal, which means to disclose, bring to light, to make known.

> Even in apparent defeat God can cause us to have the victory. Victory speaks of winning! God is a winner, Jesus is a winner and the Holy Ghost is a winner! This means that every born-again child of God is a winner whether they realize it or not.

Our revelation of complete victory in Jesus will produce the sweet fruit of joy. Victorious people are joyful people. You will never meet anyone who has won something who does not have joy. Joy is the natural by-product of victory. The more you win the more joy you will experience. So get this in your spirit now and say often "I have the victory" and "victory is mine." Because as you do so, your revelation with your faith will give birth to joy.

Scripture References

2 Corinthians 2:14; Romans 8:37; 1 John 4:4; Matthew 5:13-16

DAY 11

GOOD MEDICINE THAT WON'T COST A DIME

"Your ulcer can't grow while you are laughing!" That's what a merry heart can do for you. It will bring healing and joy that will help ease any pain you may be dealing with. The Bible makes a profound statement in Proverbs 17:22.

Proverbs 17:22 (KJV)

[22] A merry heart doeth good *like* a medicine: but a broken spirit drieth the bones.

The Holy Spirit reveals to us the therapeutic properties of joy, merriment, and laughter. He is telling us to spend more time enjoying life, especially the things that bring us joy instead of wasting valuable time and energy on the things we can't control.

> "Your ulcer can't grow while you are laughing!" That's what a merry heart can do for you. It will bring healing and joy that will help ease any pain you may be dealing with.

Ask yourself this question. What brings me joy? What can I do today that really pleases me? Am I really thankful for the family God has given me, the health that I have, the gifts and talents I possess, or the beauty and splendor of the earth that I see daily? If we would take the time to focus on the good things in life, we would have more joy.

Another key to enjoying life is not to take everything so seriously. Don't be a sour puss! Learn to laugh at life! This also means to laugh at yourself. Believe it or not you can do some funny things at times. At our home we have a little saying whenever someone trips or just does something goofy! For instance if you trip over something and someone sees you, we shout "cool points!" In other words you lose cool points for being human. Well everyone qualifies to have cool points taken away because we all make mistakes. The person who makes the mishap and the person who discovers it both end up with a hearty laugh! The Word of God is true, a merry heart does good. It's a tonic that heals, just like medicine. Remember laughter is the shock absorber that eases the blows of life.

Scripture References

Proverbs 17:22

DAY 12

YOUR TRIAL IS SEASONAL

No pain is forever! No tragedy comes to stay. Testing and trials are seasonal. In other words there is a lifespan to any situation you may be

> Faith in God will always produce a hope that will keep you expecting while you are in the tough place!

encountering. Solomon said "to everything there is a season." (Ecclesiastes 3:1) Webster describes the word season as a "period of time." Meaning that your troubles have not come to stay, but they have come to pass! Notice the how the writer in Psalms 30:5 put it.

Psalm 30:5 (KJV)

⁵ For his anger *endureth but* a moment; in his favour *is* life: weeping may endure for a night, but joy *cometh* in the morning.

What David discovered was that in spite of how bad things may get, they always tend to get better. One of the keys to outlasting your trial is to believe. Jesus said in Mark 9:23 "If thou canst believe all things are possible to him that believeth." Keep believing in the midst of your test and never, never stop believing! Faith in God will always produce a hope that will keep you expecting while you are in the tough place! Jesus told Jairus "only believe" (Mark 5:36) after he had received the worst news possible. Why would he say that? I believe He was teaching Believers today to hold on to our faith even when it looks like all hope is gone. Faith in the promises of God will always overcome any roadblock that the devil puts in your way.

David stated in Psalms 34:19 "Many are the afflictions of the righteous, but the Lord delivereth him out of them all. Seasonal. Though he fall, he shall not be utterly cast down. (Psalms 37:24) Seasonal. For a just man falleth seven times. (Proverbs 24:6) Seasonal. A great man of God said, "If you would be willing to stand forever you will always win." How about you? How long are you willing to stand until you see the victory in your trial? The Lord taught us to build our lives on His words so that when the storms of life come, we would be able to survive. Here is a word of encouragement, "if your test had a beginning, then it also has an ending." Now that's something to shout about!

Scripture References

Psalms 30:5; Mark 9:23; Mark 5:36; Psalms 34:19; Psalms 37:24; Proverbs 24:6

DAY 13

WHEN YOU FEEL DOWN AND OUT SING A SONG!

A popular secular group penned the now famous lyrics which we take today's title from. No doubt the writer was inspired by both biblical and secular teaching. But one

> Do you have a heavy heart? Then sing. Are you lonely, then sing! Experiencing financial lack or debt, then sing the Lord is my Shepard and I do not want.

thing is for sure, there is something awesome about singing! It indicates a joyful heart and a peaceful spirit. Very rarely do you find people singing who are depressed, discouraged, or angry. No, people who sing are those who are rejoicing in the midst of their circumstances. People who sing are just like people everywhere else, they have their share of test, trials, and disappointments. But they have discovered the revelation that the heart full of praise and thanksgiving is the heart that overcomes!

Ephesians 5:19 teaches us to "speak to ourselves in psalms and hymns, and spiritual songs, singing and making melody in our heart to the Lord!" Singing and making melodies sound like joy, looks like faith, and tastes like victory! All throughout the scriptures we find that singing is associated with celebrating and rejoicing. It is difficult to sing a song of joy and remain depressed and defeated! It does not matter if you sing a song of praise or if you sing an oldie goldie from your childhood, it energizes your spirit. From time to time my wife and I play name that tune and we will sing, whistle, or hum the melody to a particular song and then try to guess who the artist is or the name of the song. We always play this at night before we retire. There have been some nights where we have stayed up until three a.m., just having fun singing and making melody in our hearts. Do you have a heavy heart? Then sing. Are you lonely, then sing! Experiencing financial lack or debt, then sing the Lord is my Shepard and I do not want. The Word of God teaches us to "come into His presence with singing (Psalms 100:2) and to make joyful noises unto our God. (Psalm 100:1) Take time to read and meditate in the Psalms, which incidentally served as the song book of the children of Israel. If you would pay close attention you would discover that when they were in trouble, or oppressed they would sing their way out of danger. They would sing to remind themselves of God's faithfulness and His great mercy and power! King Jehoshaphat even put singers ahead of his armies when he went out to battle three armies larger and superior to his own and God routed his enemies. (2 Chronicles 20;21-22) Remember God lives in, abides in and dwells in the praises of His people. (Psalms 22:3). So sing about His excellence, goodness, and love and God will come on the scene and turn your mourning into dancing! (Psalms 30:11)

Scripture References

Ephesians 5:19: Psalms 100:1; Psalms 100:2; 2 Chronicles 20:21-22; Psalms 22:3: Psalms 30:11

DAY 14

JOY AND PEACE IN BELIEVING

Faith and believing are discernable. In other words you can tell who believes and who does not. Our expressions, our words, and our actions signal to others more than anything else what is really in our heart. Paul stated in Romans 15:13;

Romans 15:13 (KJV)

[13] Now the God of hope fill you with all joy and peace in believing, that ye may abound in hope, through the power of the Holy Ghost.

Paul's revelation here teaches us that where there is no joy and peace, there is also no faith! I pray that you get the picture here; joy is an expression and indicator of faith in God and His Word. The soul that is depressed, discouraged, and fearful is the soul that is devoid of faith. The heart full of joy is an expectant heart, a positive heart, an assured heart that believes all things will work out for their good! Believers have to be honest, if we are fearful, or depressed we have focused too much attention on our circumstances rather than the one who is God over our circumstances. A minister once put it this way, "faith rejoices and is glad, doubt fears and is sad." Think about it, if God has answered your prayer then you should be

> Faith and believing are discernable. In other words you can tell who believes and who does not. Our expressions, our words, and our actions signal to others more than anything else what is really in our heart.

glad, not sad! If you believe that God is for you, then you should be full of joy. Notice again what Paul said in Romans 8:31.

Romans 8:31 (KJV)

[31] What shall we then say to these things? If God *be* for us, who *can be* against us?

That means you win and winners are happy people, victorious people, confident people. Here is a question. Are you confident in the promises of God? If you are, you should be wearing the garment of praise and thanksgiving! Because you know that God will never let you down or abandon you. Your name is written in the palm of His hand. (Isaiah 49:16) So make sure your joy tank stays full.

Scripture References

Romans 15:13; Romans 8:31; Isaiah 49:16

DAY 15
BE OF GOOD CHEER

It is interesting that Jesus would use this phrase along with the thought of a crisis. John the beloved disciple quotes Him in John 16:33;

John 16:33 (KJV)

[33] These things I have spoken unto you, that in me ye might have peace. In the world ye shall have tribulation: but be of good cheer; I have overcome the world.

It looks like Jesus is saying it is important for us to keep the right mental attitude during your seasons of testing and tribulation. The right attitude is essential in surviving any adverse situation. Battles of life are won and lost due to the use or lack of the right attitude. Life should not be absent of joy when we understand the principle of victory. God is not pleased when His children are not happy and full of joy. If human parents can discern the moods of our children and grieve when they are not happy, then how much more does our heavenly Father grieve when we are not enjoying ourselves in His love and provision.

> So just as the natural storm needs strength to last or survive, so do we need strength to survive the test and trials of life. Learning to laugh at yourself, learning to be thankful even in severe disappointments and seasons, enable us to endure the onslaughts of the devil.

Here is another point to this statement. Notice that Jesus did not ask us to be of good cheer. He did not say be of good cheer when all is well, the sun is shining, and everyone speaks well of you. No, He commanded us to be of good cheer. Now our heads and the enemy will tell us it is impossible to do so. But we must realize that God will never instruct us to do something that we cannot do! He is too just for that! He is revealing to us one of the keys to outlasting the storms of life. Joy! Things in life are better when taken with a smile! When things go wrong don't get mad, but rejoice. It gives you the strength you need to make it through the crisis. Scientist will tell you that every storm needs energy to live, hurricanes, thunderstorms, tornadoes etc. Even medical science will attest to the fact that diseases, tumors, and illnesses feed and need a source of life or strength. So just as the natural storm needs strength to last or survive, so do we need strength to survive the test and trials of life. Learning to laugh at yourself, learning to be thankful even in severe disappointments and seasons, enable us to endure the onslaughts of the devil. It's about discipline, doing the right thing even when it seems like it does not make sense. Remember right things produce right results. So here is one of the keys to winning in life, be of good cheer!

Scripture References

John 16:33

DAY 16
PRAISE THE LANGUAGE OF FAITH

One of the greatest revelations I ever received was the fact that faith has a voice! If faith is in your heart it will come out of your mouth. Jesus taught this in Matthew 12:34 when He said "for out of the abundance of the heart the mouth speaketh." So our words are indicators declaring to others what we really think and feel. With our words we create languages, and with our language we communicate. I recently heard a well-known minister teach that life is a language. He went on to say that death is also a language. From this summation we can easily understand that failure, unbelief, and doubt can be languages as well. But then, there is also the language of faith, and it is called praise.

Praise is the language of champions. Champions learn early the value of praise. It has been said that whatever you praise becomes greater and better in quality! That is the power of praise. David was a champion and hero of the faith. He said in Psalms 34:1 "I will bless the Lord at all times, and His praise shall continually be in my mouth." David was a praiser and God said he was a man after his own heart. People who praise are people who believe and because they believe they live with joy in the anticipation of God coming through for them. It takes faith to praise God before we notice any tangible

> People who praise are people who believe and because they believe they live with joy in the anticipation of God coming through for them. It takes faith to praise God before we notice any tangible results.

results. Most people want to wait for the answer and then maybe give thanks, but that takes no faith. But when we offer praise in our trouble it indicates that we believe God that it shall be even as it was told to us. (Acts 27:25) So remember, live the life of praise and speak the language of faith realizing that your heavenly Father and His word will never let you down!

Scripture References

Matthew 12:34; Psalm 34:11; Acts 27:25

DAY 17
JOY TO THE WORLD

This seasonal phrase should become a constant in the hearts of believers worldwide. The birth of the Messiah inspired this wonderful song and his gift of righteousness to us should inspire us to live in joy. In a world full of (and I emphasize) depression, fear, trouble, and disappointments it is good to know that there is a source and a reason for pure joy. People wear their true emotions while doing the most mundane activities. As an example just watch the faces of people on their way to work. There are few expressions of cheerfulness and few give the impression of enjoyment. The busyness and stress associated with activities and obligations rob many of the joy that Jesus came to give freely. One minister said we need a revival of joy! I concur! Joy to the world begins when there is joy in the home.

Only then can it spread to the work place, then to the schools until it reaches every arena of life. Let's decide today to do battle against the circumstances of life by walking by faith. Calling those things that be not as though they were, rejoicing in the Lord always, maintaining the joy that only God could supply. When we do this we can then take our joy and spread it to those outside of the household of faith. The song writer

One minister said we need a revival of joy! I concur! Joy to the world begins when there is joy in the home.

Only then can it spread to the work place, then to the schools until it reaches every arena of life. Let's decide today to do battle against the circumstances of life by walking by faith. Calling those things that be not as though they were, rejoicing in the Lord always, maintaining the joy that only God could supply.

stated "joy to the world, the Lord is come. Let earth receive her King, Hallelujah! It is time for the earth to receive her king. Receive Him now; receive Him with joy and gladness. For He has come that we might have life in abundance, to the full, till it overflows and full of joy unspeakable and full of glory!**Scripture References**

Romans 4:17; John 10:10; Psalms 98

DAY 18
PUT YOUR SHOUTING CLOTHES ON

The prophet Isaiah said in Isaiah 61:3; "to appoint unto them that mourn in Zion, to give unto them beauty for ashes, the oil of joy for mourning, the garment of praise for the spirit of heaviness." God sent His son Jesus to give us beauty for ashes, the oil of joy and the garment of praise for a heavy failing spirit. Too often instead of wearing the garment of praise, we are often found wallowing in the spirit of heaviness. Instead of crying over spilled milk, playing into the hand of the enemy of our joy, we should put on our garment of praise in the midst our adversity. The phrase "do you have your shouting clothes on" comes from the idea that some garments are suited for jumping and shouting in the

> Too often instead of wearing the garment of praise, we are often found wallowing in the spirit of heaviness. Instead of crying over spilled milk, playing into the hand of the enemy of our joy, we should put on our garment of praise in the midst our adversity.

minds of many. But the garment of praise does not fit in that category, it is proper for any occasion or environment. When things are fine, it's proper, when things are bad and the weather is cloudy it is proper! You don't have to worry about it tearing or stretching because it is made by the universe's greatest tailor and the fabric is supernatural! It even has the power to change how a person feels and reacts. Yes it's your shouting clothes and they never wear out. They look great in the home, on the job, sharp in the church, and classy while in the mall. So when the spirit of heaviness touches you on the shoulder just turn around and show it your praise gear made by Jesus.

Scripture References

Isaiah 61:3

DAY 19

THE WORLD CAN'T
TAKE IT AWAY

Jesus said in John 16:22 "your joy no man taketh away from you." Let's look at that verse in its entirety.

What joy bubbles up in our hearts when we know the King of Kings and the Lord of Lords is coming to our rescue. It's a supernatural joy that no devil, demon, or man can take away from you.

John 16:22 (KJV)

²² And ye now therefore have sorrow: but I will see you again, and your heart shall rejoice, and your joy no man taketh from you.

Satan is the thief of joy. His weapon of discouragement is designed to keep the child of God down, defeated, discouraged, and disappointed. Sickness and disease seeks to rob you of health and long life. Poverty desires to rob you of the joy of experiencing the abundant life. But joy that comes from Jesus is an everlasting, never ending perpetual joy. Jesus taught that His return would produce rejoicing that would never fade away.

Someone wrote "when we all get to heaven what a day of rejoicing that will be!" Jesus has promised to return for us all one day. In His departure His followers were saddened, but He promised in His return their mourning would turn into joy. I also like what is said in John 14:18;

John 14:18 (KJV)

[18] I will not leave you comfortless: I will come to you.

His return is not just reserved for the rapture and the second coming, but it also means He will come to us in a day of affliction, trouble, or anxiety. What joy bubbles up in our hearts when we know the King of Kings and the Lord of Lords is coming to our rescue. It's a supernatural joy that no devil demon, or man can take away from you. Even in adverse times, moral impurity, and economic decline there is a joy that comes only from God that enables us to endure the storms of life!

Scripture References

John 16:22; John 14:18

DAY 20
JOY COMETH

Thank God, that wherever there is sorrow or disappointment, joy is not far behind. David said "weeping (sorrow) may endure for a night, but joy cometh in the morning. (Psalms 30:5) The

> But I have learned that every test has a life span. No problem or circumstance can last forever. Only the Word of God endures and exists forever. Paul put it this way, "for our light affliction which is but for a moment. (2 Corinthian 4:17)

morning represents our hope for a better day and a better future. Hope, which is confident expectation, is the blueprint for our faith in our never failing God to see us through. The night represents our many setbacks, disappointments, and failure. But I have learned that every test has a life span. No problem or circumstance can last forever. Only the Word of God endures and exists forever. Paul put it this way, "for our light affliction which is but for a moment. (2 Corinthian 4:17) The afflictions of life are but for a moment, and Paul continues in verse 18 by explaining that we don't focus our thoughts and attention on the things we see, because they are temporary or temporal. Thank God our problems did not come to stay, but they came to pass! Passing out of our lives ushering in the joy that comes in the morning. Notice that weeping and night are companions, but joy and morning are also companions. The morning represents that which is new, refreshing, and exhilarating. It ushers in our deliverance and relief from the oppression of the night. Where there is morning you will find the godly companion of joy. So rejoice for this is the day that the Lord has made, and I will rejoice and be glad in it. (Psalms118:24)

Psalm 118:24 (KJV)

[24] This *is* the day *which* the Lord hath made; we will rejoice and be glad in it.

If the Word declares that joy cometh in the morning, then we need to begin declaring that "it's morning time!" Right now! Today is our day of salvation because joy comes with the beginning of each new day!

Scripture References

Psalms 30:5; 2 Corinthians 4:17; Psalms 118:24

DAY 21
CHANGE YOUR OIL

Automobile engineers teach us to change our oil every 3,000 miles or so. Most of us (at least from my generation) can remember the mechanic who comments "you can pay me now, or you can pay me later." Changing your oil on a regular basis is preventive maintenance that will add to the life of your engine.

In the same way, believers need regular oil changes spiritually to stay on top of their game so to speak. Now the obvious question is what kind of oil are you referring to? I am referring to the oil of the Holy Ghost.

How can we change our oil? Well Isaiah also spoke of the garment of praise. Garments are indicative of mood changes. In the Bible garments represented class, status, and emotions. Blind Bartimaeus threw off his beggars garment in anticipation of receiving his sight. (Mark 10) Likewise we should learn to praise God in our sorrows, for then and only then will the oil of joy lubricate our circumstances and take away the daily grind that eats away at our heart. Our thankfulness in the winter and silent seasons of our lives will determine our outcome from that which has been sent to hinder us. So remember a smart owner realizes that he must change his oil consistently. Don't allow

> Isaiah preached about Jesus who would come to give us beauty for ashes, the oil of joy for mourning, the garment of praise for the spirit heaviness. (Isaiah 61:3) God provided the oil of joy for those who mourn! Life's tragedies, and disappointments, and failures may cause us to drop our heads in despair, but Jesus came with the remedy for life's unexpected events, the oil of joy!

your spiritual oil to become weak, dirty, lacking the viscosity it needs to do the job. Stay on top of your game. Change your oil.

Scripture References

Isaiah 61:3; Mark 10:46-52

DAY 22
FILLED WITH LAUGHTER

In too many places in our world today people are filled with too much of the wrong things. Men today are filled with hatred, violence, alcohol, drugs, fear, and other things that vex the soul and destroy the basis of life and happiness that is meant for everyone. The selfishness of men drives them to win or succeed at any cost and even after reaching their lofty and carnal goals they find themselves filled with emptiness instead of joy. This way of living produces people who become misers who are ungrateful and angry. These people never learn to enjoy the gift of life, so consequently they lack one of God's greatest gifts to the world! Laughter!

In a day and age where many are in tears due to poverty, famine, and deception we need to relearn the childlike trait of laughing! One sure indication that something is wrong with

> I believe that Jesus laughed often; I don't believe He went around like a stuffed shirt always barking out orders. He was fun to be around on top of the fact that His teachings were brilliant and revelatory.

a child is to notice the absence of laughter. As a matter of fact, laughter and play are synonymous. Because where there is play there is laughter. We all know the saying "all work and no play make Jack a dull boy." Some Christians believe that salvation means that we can't play anymore. So they go around carrying the burden of the world on their shoulders and they chide anyone else who dare to walk in faith, trusting that God is able to perform His word and hear and answer prayer. Remember this, free people are happy people, joyful people are faith people, and prosperous victorious people are laughing people. I believe that Jesus laughed often; I don't believe He went around like a stuffed shirt always barking out orders. He was fun to be around on top of the fact that His teachings were brilliant and revelatory. Ask yourself a question, when was the last time you had a good laugh? Someone said "people tend to avoid me." Sure, because you are not fun to be around. Take note of people who smile and laugh and often, they're attractive. People are drawn towards them. When you are filled with laughter you are filled with God's Spirit.

Scripture References

Psalms 126:1-2

DAY 23
DANCE THE NIGHT AWAY

When the joy of the Lord is upon you, you can really dance the night away. Dancing is an indication of enjoyment and celebration. When good things happen people often express their happiness in the dance. Dancing is not evil; it does not come from the enemy. It is a gift from God. After the Egyptians were defeated by God at the Red Sea, the Word of God states,

Exodus 15:20 (KJV)

20 And Miriam the prophetess, the sister of Aaron, took a timbrel in her hand; and all the women went out after her with timbrels and with dances.

David followed the same example when the Ark of the Covenant was brought back to Jerusalem, the Bible said David danced before the Lord with all his might. (1 Samuel 6:14) Another translation states that "he danced with great abandonment before the Lord.

> When the joy of the Lord is upon you, you can really dance the night away. Dancing is an indication of enjoyment and celebration. When good things happen people often express their happiness in the dance. Dancing is not evil; it does not come from the enemy. It is a gift from God.

That's the testimony we should desire to have, one of joy and celebration. Someone should be able to say "we danced out of our minds before the Lord!" What time is it in your life? Is it a day when you can see the brilliance of the glory of God in every area of your life or is it night where there is confusion, disappointment, and fear? What should we do in the night hour, during the darkest time in our lives. Well Paul and Silas prayed and sang praises and their deliverance came. I am inclined to believe that if it's ok to praise God at midnight, then it is also appropriate to dance the night away. Instead of throwing a pity party, with gloom, despair, and agony on me, begin to celebrate with a trusting heart believing that you have received according to Mark 11:24! Believing produces joy which should lead to celebration expressed in a holy heartfelt thankfulness to the Lord!

Scripture References

Exodus 15:20; 1 Samuel 6:14; Acts 16:25; Mark 11:24

DAY 24
DIVINE ENCOUNTERS

Isaiah 64:5 (KJV)

[5] Thou meetest him that rejoiceth and worketh righteousness, *those that* remember thee in thy ways: behold, thou art wroth; for we have sinned: in those is continuance, and we shall be saved.

Notice the first part of that verse, what a statement! The prophet is literally saying that God communes, meets with, and makes his abode around those who rejoice. Many people who wonder what it takes to have the presence of God on them continually might well take note of this verse. God loves the happy heart! He loves the heart full of praise and adoration for Him and creation. I am reminded of Psalms 91:15 where God promises to be with us in trouble.

Psalm 91:15 (KJV)

[15] He shall call upon me, and I will answer him: I *will be* with him in trouble; I will deliver him, and honour him.

> Notice the first part of that verse, what a statement! The prophet is literally saying that God communes, meets with, and makes his abode around those who rejoice. Many people who wonder what it takes to have the presence of God on them continually might well take note of this verse. God loves the happy heart! He loves the heart full of praise and adoration for Him and creation

Honestly the last thing we want to do when we are in trouble is to rejoice. As a matter of fact Jesus said in Matthew 5:11-12;

Matthew 5:11-12 (KJV)

[11] Blessed are ye, when *men* shall revile you, and persecute *you*, and shall say all manner of evil against you falsely, for my sake.

[12] Rejoice, and be exceeding glad: for great *is* your reward in heaven: for so persecuted they the prophets which were before you.

Did you ever wonder why the Lord is encouraging us to rejoice in times of trouble? Well I believe Isaiah gives us the key in chapter 64 verse 15. God will meet us there when we decide to rejoice! So if it is trouble, bad news, or persecution, God promises to show up where there is rejoicing and thanksgiving. The Amplified Bible puts it this way, "You meet and spare him who joyfully works righteousness." Did you notice the phrase "spare him?" Spare him from what? The snare of the fowler that's what! Because we choose to rejoice God promises to spare us from the judgments of this world. Here is truly the heart of God, He never desires his children to suffer wrath. He seeks to deliver, and He seeks to set the captive free! So rejoice and you will encounter a holy visitation of His Spirit.

Scripture Reference

Isaiah 64:5; Psalms 91:15; Matthew 5:11-12

DAY 25
REJOICE IN THE LORD ALWAYS

The Bible is a book of commandments, not suggestions from God! Many Christians have assumed that God has only suggested that we walk in love, turn the other cheek, or call those things that be not as though they were. But the Lord has given us specific instructions on how we are to conduct ourselves in matters pertaining to everyday life. Philippians 4:7 is another example of His commandments;

Philippians 4:4 (KJV)

⁴ Rejoice in the Lord alway: *and* again I say, Rejoice.

Notice His emphasis on rejoicing. He emphasizes the importance of maintaining a heart of joy. The person who lives by this rule walks in an anointing that will put him over in every test and trial that comes his way. Strength, power, force, vigor, intestinal fortitude, endurance, durability, these things come with joy according to Nehemiah 8:10. God commands us to rejoice so that we can maintain the strength needed to overcome the troubles of life. The Holy Spirit revealed it to me this way; we outlast trials, we pass test, we overcome obstacles and we resist temptations.

The key to victory is rejoicing at all times. No matter how bad things may seem. We have to develop a lifestyle of praise

> The person who lives by this rule walks in an anointing that will put him over in every test and trial that comes his way.

and thanksgiving that will express the joy of the Lord. Paul was in a Roman jail where it might have been damp, dark, and dreary. With the enemy putting thoughts of despair in his head, he allowed his inner man to rise up and pen one of the most loved and cherished verses in the New Testament.

Acts 16:25 (KJV)

[25] And at midnight Paul and Silas prayed, and sang praises unto God: and the prisoners heard them.

Here is a great example of what we should do when midnight comes into our lives and victory seems to be lost. Notice that Paul and Silas prayed and sang praises in the worst of circumstances. They were in jail, but they did not let the jail get in them! I think they have taught us how to keep the faith when the storms of life roll in. Rejoice in the Lord at all times!

Scripture References

Philippians 4:4; Acts 16:25; Nehemiah 8:10

DAY 26

AT MIDNIGHT

Midnight, the darkest point of the evening, the time where darkness reaches its full potential. It can be a time of horror and fear, and a time of confusion, nevertheless it is a segment of time that must be dealt with. The Bible tells of a story concerning two men traveling to preach the Word of God when the Church was in its infancy. When you study the 16th chapter of Acts you will discover that Paul and Silas initially chose to carry their ministry in other directions. But each time they made a choice they were divinely redirected until one fateful night Paul saw in a vision a man who invited him into Greece to a region called Macedonia. While they was there they faithfully preached the Word, led a woman to the Lord, and later they cast out an evil spirit in a young girl who had a spirit of fortune telling. Now you would think that the people and town would be rejoicing over this display of the power of God. But the very opposite occurred, the people were angry over their loss of income due to Paul's antics of exorcism concerning the young girl, violently took hold of Paul and Silas and brought them before the authorities. Who in turn had them both beaten and cast into the inner most part of the prison. For most Christians it would have been "crying time again." Most Christians would begin to question the integrity of

> But what Paul and Silas did raised the bar for all eternity. Instead of meditating on their problems they chose to meditate on their savior. History records their act of faith with the statement "at midnight Paul and Silas prayed and sang praises unto God."

51

Almighty God. Focusing on the circumstances many would become angry with God instead of trusting His Word to never abandon them.

But what Paul and Silas did raised the bar for all eternity. Instead of meditating on their problems they chose to meditate on their savior. History records their act of faith with the statement "at midnight Paul and Silas prayed and sang praises unto God."

Acts 16:25 (KJV)

[25] And at midnight Paul and Silas prayed, and sang praises unto God: and the prisoners heard them.

They decided to bless God instead of cursing him! In spite of all their pain and suffering, disappointments, and questions they had determined that God was still worthy of praise and glory! They determined that even though they were in prison, they were not going to let the prison get in them! Their worship and praise not only liberated their spirits but it also liberated their bodies! God was so pleased by their sacrifice of praise that He delivered them through a mighty earthquake! We have to remember that deliverance is always around the corner where there is praise and worship. So the next time you find yourself in a spiritual or natural prison don't murmur and complain, open you mouth and bless the Lord!

Scripture References

Acts 16:24; Psalms 34:1

FIRE SHUT UP IN MY BONES

What Jeremiah alluded to in Jeremiah 20:9 was an inward conviction that would not allow him to retreat from his calling.

Jeremiah 20:9 (KJV)

⁹ Then I said, I will not make mention of him, nor speak any more in his name. But *his word* was in mine heart as a burning fire shut up in my bones, and I was weary with forbearing, and I could not *stay*.

So too is the conviction from men of character and integrity who forge ahead in their work for God and man in spite of their challenges. Men in this category have an inward conviction that compels them to keep the dream alive! Let's consider this man for a moment. Would you consider him a coward? Of course not! How about being a man of timidity and insecurity? Certainly not! Could he be a person full of sadness and depression? Could he "toe the line" so to speak if his spirits were low? Would he be bold enough to utter a statement such as Jeremiah's if he was a man who talked and acted like a victim instead of a champ?

> So too is the conviction from men of character and integrity who forge ahead in their work for God and man in spite of their challenges. Men in this category have an inward conviction that compels them to keep the dream alive

The short answer is no. Men of woe never rise above the level of their emotions. Since they have no faith they display no joy. The fire of God's Word will always produce the fruit of joy. Jeremiah's statement does not speak of joy directly, but we realize that to obey God's calling is to experience a joy like no other. John said that His commandments were not greivious (1 John 5:3). There is joy in preaching the Word, there is joy in rededicating your life to do the will of God! Obeying and relinquishing his own will, brought joy and excitement to Jeremiah's ministry. It will do the same for you. Stay at it, never even consider for a moment thought of quitting. Remember there is joy and peace in the will of God.

Scripture References

Jeremiah 20:9; 1 John 5:3

DAY 28
IT'S TIME TO RELOCATE

In the world when a neighborhood deteriorates it is a natural thing to relocate your family and move to a better community. The benefits are obvious, you distance yourself from the greater threat of burglary, violent crime, and you

> Choices and decisions, they can either make us or break us. Our choices will determine our level of success or failure in the game of life. Refuse to remain in situations that foster attitudes and feelings that are not in line with a thankful, hopeful, and expectant heart.

place yourself in an environment conducive to better living. No one would fault you for making a bold move such as this. As a matter of fact the Word of God cautions us against bad company. Notice what Paul taught in 1 Corinthians 15:33;

1 Corinthians 15:33 (KJV)

[33] Be not deceived: evil communications corrupt good manners.

In other words wrong people or wrong places can be detrimental to your future and your dreams.

Well we can easily see the wisdom behind the behavior when it comes to natural living. But many cannot see the value of moving away from murmuring, discouragement, and criticism that poses the same threat spiritually that a bad neighborhood does naturally. So many Christians choose to live on Grumble Alley, instead of enjoying life on Praise Avenue. Let's face it, anybody can complain and make excuses, but it takes maturity to look past offenses and disappointments so that life can be enjoyed instead of just tolerated. Choices and decisions, they can either make us or break us. Our choices will determine our level of success or failure in the game of life. Refuse to remain in situations that foster attitudes and feelings that are not in line with a thankful, hopeful, and expectant heart. One of the greatest gifts given to mankind is the ability to choose. You don't have to stay where you are, live in the past or resign yourself to some hopeless state of existence. Make that move to a place where the praise produces peace, and the peace results in a joy that's unspeakable and full of glory.

Scripture References

1 Corinthians 15:33

THE DEVIL IS A LIAR

Simply stated a liar is one who speaks that which is untrue. He or she is a person you can't trust, a person void of character and fidelity. People to stay away from, because he can only cause you harm. So who would believe a liar? Let's take this a step further; who even in their right mind would even talk to a liar? I'll tell you who, Christians would! Never mind the fact that they know that Jesus called the devil a liar and the father of liars. (John 8:44) Jesus said he was a liar from the beginning. So why would you get upset about anything he said? Remember those who break bread with the devil will always end up with heart-burn! Is the devil saying things about you such as: "you will never make it", "you are going to die", "nobody likes you", or "you are not good enough?"

If so, then begin to shout and rejoice because based on his track record, you are going to get the exact opposite of what he said! Never entertain his thoughts or suggestions. Paul instructed us to bring every thought into captivity.

> **Negative thoughts produce doubt and despair in the lives of believers. Recognize the source of every debilitating desire or thought. James said that we should resist the devil and he (the devil) would flee from us. (James 4:7) Resist anything that would rob you of the joy of believing.**

2 Corinthians 10:4-5 (KJV)

[4] (For the weapons of our warfare *are* not carnal, but mighty through God to the pulling down of strong holds;)

[5] Casting down imaginations, and every high thing that exalteth itself against the knowledge of God, and bringing into captivity every thought to the obedience of Christ;

Negative thoughts produce doubt and despair in the lives of believers. Recognize the source of every debilitating desire or thought. James said that we should resist the devil and he (the devil) would flee from us. (James 4:7) Resist anything that would rob you of the joy of believing.

Scripture References (John 8:44; 2Corinthians 10:4; James 4:7)

DAY 30
STAY IN HIS PRESENCE

Joy is a supernatural force from God that can dominate and overthrow every test or trail that you may face. A key to maintaining this supernatural force is found in Psalms 16:11.

Psalm 16:11 (KJV)

[11] Thou wilt shew me the path of life: in thy presence *is* fulness of joy; at thy right hand *there are* pleasures for evermore.

According to what David said the Lord will show us the path of life. This path or place of life is what every child of God desires, the path where we walk in the fullness of all that belongs to us. Now notice the next phrase "in thy presence", here is the key to what the psalmist is trying to get across to us. If we want to stay full of God and what the world has to offer, then we must live in his presence! Staying full of God would mean staying full of all that He has to offer, including His joy! There in His presence is a fullness of joy, completeness, abundance, and a total satisfaction of joy. But the key to maintaining this supernatural force seems to lie in our own ability to stay in His presence. To the degree

> Staying full of God would mean staying full of all that He has to offer, including His joy! There in His presence is a fullness of joy, completeness, abundance, and a total satisfaction of joy. But the key to maintaining this supernatural force seems to lie in our own ability to stay in His presence.

that we learn to live in His presence daily will be the degree that we will experience His joy. I heard a minister state that we should practice the presence of God. In other words practice His presence in our everyday living. We don't have to be in a posture of prayer, or in a bible study or around other saints. We can experience God's presence in every situation or circumstance. Besides that's where and when we really need the joy of the Lord, on the job, in our homes, in the market place, and with other people! If we learn to stay in His presence our joy will always be apparent and overflowing.

Scripture References

Psalms 16:11

DAY 31

THAT YOUR JOY
MIGHT BY FULL

Jesus encouraged the disciples to pray. In Luke 18:1 He said, "Men ought to pray always and faint or give up. Notice what He also taught in John 15:7:

John 15:7 (KJV)

[7] If ye abide in me, and my words abide in you, ye shall ask what ye will, and it shall be done unto you.

So we see a pattern of instruction in the ministry of Jesus to place a special emphasis on prayer. One vital aspect is asking. Now some have misused this aspect by only practicing it to the demise of other facets of prayer. Nevertheless prayer would not be prayer without the principle of asking. Now Jesus said in John 16:24.."ask and ye shall receive, that your joy might be full." We see that joy comes from receiving the answer or the result of prayer. Make no doubt about it, God desires his children to be joyful, happy, and hilarious. Living a carefree life and walking in the light of our inheritance in Him. John Wesley's statement comes to mind concerning our part in the affairs of men on the earth. He stated, "It seems like God is limited by our prayer lives, He can only do

> We see that joy comes from receiving the answer or the result of prayer. Make no doubt about it, God desires his children to be joyful, happy, and hilarious. Living a carefree life and walking in the light of our inheritance in Him.

for humanity what we ask Him to." Well when we ask Him to perform His will on the earth, the Church of Jesus Christ is going to get some joy! When we as individuals ask God to move in our homes, communities, and nations the result will be God's kingdom manifesting on the earth producing a peace and joy that we can only imagine. James teaches in chapter four that "we have not because we ask not, so let's not forfeit our joy by neglecting to ask our heavenly Father to move in our lives.

Scripture References

John 15:7; John16:24

ABOUT THE AUTHOR

Rev. Michael G. Crenshaw is a born again Spirit-filled man of God who was born and raised in Birmingham, Alabama. He is married to Phyllis McCray-Crenshaw his wife of nearly thirty years. They have three sons Michael, Hilton, and Ashton. Brother Michael studied at Alabama A&M University and Rhema Bible Training Center. He has been in the ministry for almost 29 years. He is the founder of People of God Ministries in Huntsville, Alabama. For more information about Brother Michael or his ministry you can go to his website at www.peopleofgodministries.com or contact him by letter at People of God Ministries

P.O. Box 208

Normal, AL 35762

Printed in the United States
By Bookmasters